Be COMPLETELY COMFORTABLE *with the* UNIQUE WAY *God* MADE YOU

by Mary Hooks

Be Completely Comfortable with the Unique Way God made You

Copyright © 2018 by Mary Hooks

ISBN: 978-1-7327227-4-3

Printed in the United States of America

His Glory Creations Publishing, LLC

Wendell, North Carolina

www.hisglorycreationspublishing.com

This book is dedicated to young women who are battling with self-esteem issues, lack of confidence, and insecurities.

Contents

Acknowledgements

I would first like to say thank you to the Lord Jesus Christ for allowing me to make it through my mess and now have a message to share with the world.

My motivation: my two beautiful children Nevaeh Gardner and Alex McDowell Jr. for being so patient and understanding with me as I reach the masses.

Introduction

Hey, beautiful. Do you feel alone? Confused about who you are? Or maybe you don't fit in. In a room full of people you feel as if you are the outcast, no one can relate to you. Oftentimes you find yourself doing things that the real you would not do just to be accepted. Acting and dressing a certain way so you can feel as if you belong. I understand. I was you, scared to walk boldly in my uniqueness, so I pretended to be everything else other than myself and allowed other people to determine who they thought I should be. Take a walk with me through my life as I show you how not being true to who I was spun my life into a destructive whirlwind.

Authentic Traits

A ll through school I was an A/B student, a very respectful kid, and had a heart for helping others, that was up until about the seventh grade. I was active in basketball and cheerleading, and always willing to volunteer whenever needed. Seventh grade year, I started to notice that I was the oddball, the nerd, the teacher's pet as the other students would say. I found myself being teased because I was skinny; all the other girls my age were starting to develop, but not me. I didn't even need to wear a bra. I've heard it all, "You so skinny you can hula hoop through a cheerio." Not only was I very small framed, but I would always be sitting somewhere with my glasses on, reading a book. I loved to expand my mind and guys would not want to talk to me because I was always focused on my schoolwork.

I noticed that the boys liked the girls that barely came to school and when they did show up, they goofed off all day. Around this time, puberty was kicking in and I wanted a "boyfriend," which is absolutely humanly normal to feel this way. I began to long for male attention. My father lived in the same household as me. He was always gone; I saw him about four hours each day. I kind of felt neglected due to his lack of presence in the home. Every little girl wants their father around to have that bond. A father is supposed to be our hero, our protector, our first example of love. Now don't get me wrong, I love my father dearly, but I wish he would have been around more to lead and show me the things that little girls are supposed to learn from their father.

Seeking to fill that void in my life, I made the decision to slack off on my schoolwork and goof off too. Taking on the actions of what I saw others do to get the kind of attention I wanted from boys was the beginning of my downfall in life. I completely lost myself; my true self. Although I was getting more than enough attention, I was pretending to be someone I wasn't. On top of that, I was acting out of hurt.

The Switch

I came to the decision within myself that I was done being picked on and talked about. I broke my glasses, I stopped reading regularly, and I started fighting. Half the time I didn't even know what I was fighting about. I can't even tell you how many times I was suspended from school. My teachers and principal would ask me what's wrong, even my mother did, but I never gave them an answer.

I was done being Mary. Now that I had taken on this new me, a whole new personality, my alter ego, I called her "Tudie." Not only was I getting attention from boys, but from everybody. It seemed like everybody wanted to be Tudie's friend. I had to continue to be this character to fit in. Tudie was something else. She became addicted to the fame, and that led her to go deeper and deeper into sin. She became very promiscuous freshman year of high school. Skipping school to have sex with different guys, being introduced to weed, fell in love with the feeling of being high, becoming addicted, and things got worse from there. She would get on the bus to go to school just to meet up with friends and walk right back out of the building to get high.

Coming in the house at almost 12 midnight on a school night, hanging with people who did not care about her well-being only pushed her further into the streetlife. All the partying and hanging out, I thought I was having the time of my life, little did I know, I was being used. I was a human puppet moving to the strings that my so-called friends controlled. At the age of 15 years old, I became pregnant with my daughter. When I first found out, I remember I had no thought. My mind was blank. A girl friend of mine went with me to the clinic and she kept saying "What you going to do?" I responded, "Smoke this blunt." I told my mom the same day, well actually my cousin did. I felt no need to hide my child and knew that it was God's plan. I told her father and he had no thought either. We were both babies ourselves.

Being pregnant slowed me down a little bit though, I was always tired. My child's father and I would have conversations about how we were going to be a happy family, that all changed when I found out I was being cheated on all throughout my pregnancy. He decided that he didn't want to be a father, so we stopped communicating all together when our child was three months old; and I never looked back. I made a vow to myself that I would never let another man have one up on me again.

Sophomore year I dropped out of school. I suffered really bad from postpartum depression, I would lay in the bed all day long not wanting to be bothered with anyone, not even my own child. I am thankful that I had a mother and sisters that were willing to help me out and care for my baby at this dark time in my life. When you have a child with someone, you never think that you would be the only one stepping up and handling all the responsibility. I felt the only way I could be happy is by smoking weed to numb reality that I was going to be raising my child on my own. It was not easy, just a baby myself, I knew I had to make something happen.

I began working at McDonald's barely part-time, taking two buses there and back; I was basically working for bus fair. I just knew it had to be more to life than this. I felt stuck and trapped and the baby was here to stay. I quit my job. Now I'm not making any money, but I knew people that would make sure I stayed high. Be watchful of people that will support your bad habits but won't encourage you to do better. Those people like seeing you down and out and struggling, real friends are going to build you up and tell you to get yourself together.

Listen lady, do you see how quickly I went from an honor roll student to a drug addict teen mom trying to be someone I was not, trading in my core values for a counterfeit to fit in?

Oh but it didn't stop there, I eventually went back to school. I knew that I needed at least my high school diploma, so that was a goal I set out to accomplish. Back in school hanging with the same crowd skipping school, smoking, and having sex, nothing changed much, but the fact that I was introduced to alcohol and quickly became an alcoholic.

Now at this point, I began living with different friends and had pretty much walked away from motherhood. My daughter was back and forth living between my mom and her great grandmother's house. Chasing after the feeling of not being alone and now trying to fill a void because I was running from myself. A friend of mine introduced me to ecstasy which is an upper drug, so I would go days without sleep turnt up partying. I used these substances as an escape from reality. While I was intoxicated, I didn't think about my problems, I was in a daze.

I took on other people's characteristics and attitudes just to be accepted. I cared more about what other people wanted than what I wanted. I was always going out of my way to make other people happy in a way that was neglecting and harmful to me. I remember I received a phone call from a close friend of mine, she told me that she had ran into someone and we were about to get some money.

Now at this time, I had multiple addictions and I was a mom. I was down for whatever. A few days later, I met this someone she was telling me about and it turns out he was a pimp. Knowing this was not the right thing to do because I was raised better, I stayed away from my parents. I didn't want them to find out what I was getting myself into. See when we are making decisions that we know are not the right decisions, we tend to stay away from the people that we know will talk us out of it.

When I met him, he was everything I ever wanted: older guy, nice car, house, money, and rolled blunt after blunt with him telling me how he could show me a whole new lifestyle, and we were going to be rich. Without hesitation, I told him I was all in. I moved in with him and I was indeed living a whole different lifestyle. He showed me the game, taught me how to deal with my clients, to always be in control, and get the money first.

This new attention I was now receiving from him was amazing. He made me feel wanted and kept a smile on my face, we would laugh and talk, his personality and swag were perfect to me. He began to tell me things like, "I'm the only person that cares about you," and I truly started to believe that. He kept me isolated from my friends and family, so he could continue to manipulate me and have control over my every move. This was the new norm for me, traveling to different cities stripping and prostituting in and out of hotels.

At only 17 years old, I was living such a fast life while other girls my age were worrying about prom and things of that nature, I was worrying about not getting caught or set up by an undercover cop. My life was pretty wild, but I was too far in to get out now. The decisions we make in life have a big impact on the way our life turns out. If I had been in my right mind, I would have never gone that far, but I had lost her long ago when I made the decision that being true to myself was not good enough.

My senior year in high school, I was dancing at a club called Hillside. I was exposed to more and more of this lifestyle. Making fast money, hair and nails stayed done, addictions were always supplied. This was the life, I thought. Life was like one big party that never ended. I turned 18, graduated from high school, and the day after my birthday, the next thing I knew, I was headed to Miami.

Miami showed me how serious the game was. I saw other prostitutes beaten by their pimps until they were covered in blood and they acted as if it was normal because they were so used to it. When I saw this, I told my pimp if you ever put your hands on me there would be problems. Not knowing that just a week later he would begin to beat me the same way, punching me down to the floor and stomping me in my head repeatedly. Walking around with black eyes and bruises, I began applying makeup, so no one would notice. I still went out on South Beach in pain to get his money. Strip clubs by day, South Beach by night. Sleep, you ask? There was no sleep. I would be up for weeks at a time chasing after the love of money. In the strip clubs, anything goes, from drugs to sex and anything else in between. Don't ever say what you won't do in this lifestyle. The love of money will have you doing it all.

I was introduced to a drug called Molly, a much stronger version of ecstasy. It's easy to get hooked on drugs in this industry. Outside of a sober mind, performing these acts didn't seem so bad. I have done everything except shoot a needle in my arm. Having so many different sexual partners, some even old enough to be my great grandfather, and all different races; as long as they had money, it was a go.

I honestly don't know how many people I've had sex with, but I do thank God that I didn't catch any disease. Everyone involved in the game is not fortunate enough to say the same. I knew of a few women that contracted some things that are incurable and they will live with that for the rest of their lives. This is a dangerous game, seeing another prostitute out in the same streets I was in, turning tricks just like I was, and find out the next day that she was killed by a John. I was thinking to myself how that could have been me. Once again, everyone is not fortunate enough to make it out of this lifestyle, some people die in it. Others are still stuck in it at 40+ years old. This is all they know, because they were trafficked in at such a young age, it has become their career.

I called my daughter and family every now and then just to let them know I was okay. My daughter was calling me by my first name. I was missing out on the most precious moments of her life. I didn't know at the time how bad I was hurting my family. At this time, they had an idea of what I was doing and my father wouldn't even speak to me when I did call. Growing up, at times when my father was around, he would talk to me about Jesus and righteousness, so I definitely knew I was outside the will of God, but the devil had a mean grip on me and wasn't letting up. Even in my sin, I would pray because that was my foundation on the way I was raised. I knew that God was real and that He heard me. I wanted out but couldn't get out on my own. This type of thing is like a gang, once you're in, you are in it for life.

It's only by God's grace that I did make it out alive and am able to share my experiences, so you don't have to make the same mistakes I did and experience such a tough and bumpy road. I believe the only reason I did make it out is to show other young girls that the grass is not greener on the other side.

#Be Yourself

Whether your hair is long or short brown or blonde, it doesn't matter if you are fat or skinny, white or black, God intentionally created you to be that way. So be confident in it. Walk boldly in who you are, how you look, the way you talk, the flaws and all. There is no one else on this earth like you and that's the best part about being you, you bring something different and rare to the world. Just think about it, if everyone looked and acted the same way; this world would be very dull. There would be no creativity. Without each person's uniqueness, there would not be different styles of music, fashion, or art. We wouldn't be able to tell each other apart. Your uniqueness sets out your identity.

Dear Young Queen,

You are enough. Hold your head up so that your crown won't fall and strive for greatness. I oftentimes hear people say the sky is the limit, but I say the mindset is the limit. Your mind is the most powerful possession you own. What you think and focus on with your mind expands. You become what you focus on. SO everyday look in the mirror at yourself and tell yourself, "Girl you are beautiful, you are a leader, you are strong, you are courageous. What you focus on is what you find. Imagine yourself as a CEO of a million-dollar corporation or a beautician, whatever it is that your heart desire. You are strong enough to achieve anything you put your mind to, and you will only get stronger as you move forward. If nobody else is cheering for you, I AM, I BELIEVE IN YOU!

I've learned over my lifetime, people are going to talk about you whether you are doing good or bad. It is not your job to force people to like and accept you, just be your best self and the people that are meant to be in your life will come. You and your swag are just what the world needs, don't hold back!

About the Author

MARY HOOKS grew up in Milwaukee, Wisconsin where the streetlife tried to take her out. She was a teen mom involved in sex trafficking, drug/alcoholism, and domestic violence. What the enemy meant for evil, God turned for good. Today, Mary's mission is to help young women that are battling with the same issues she has overcome, as well as prevent others from falling into such a dark lifestyle. She is a motivational / enpowerment speaker and author. Saved by God's grace. Through her testimony, Mary inspires, encourages, and motivates others to be completely comfortable with the unique way God created them.

Contact information:

Email:
hooksmary49@gmail.com

Instagram:
maryhooks18

My Queen Journal

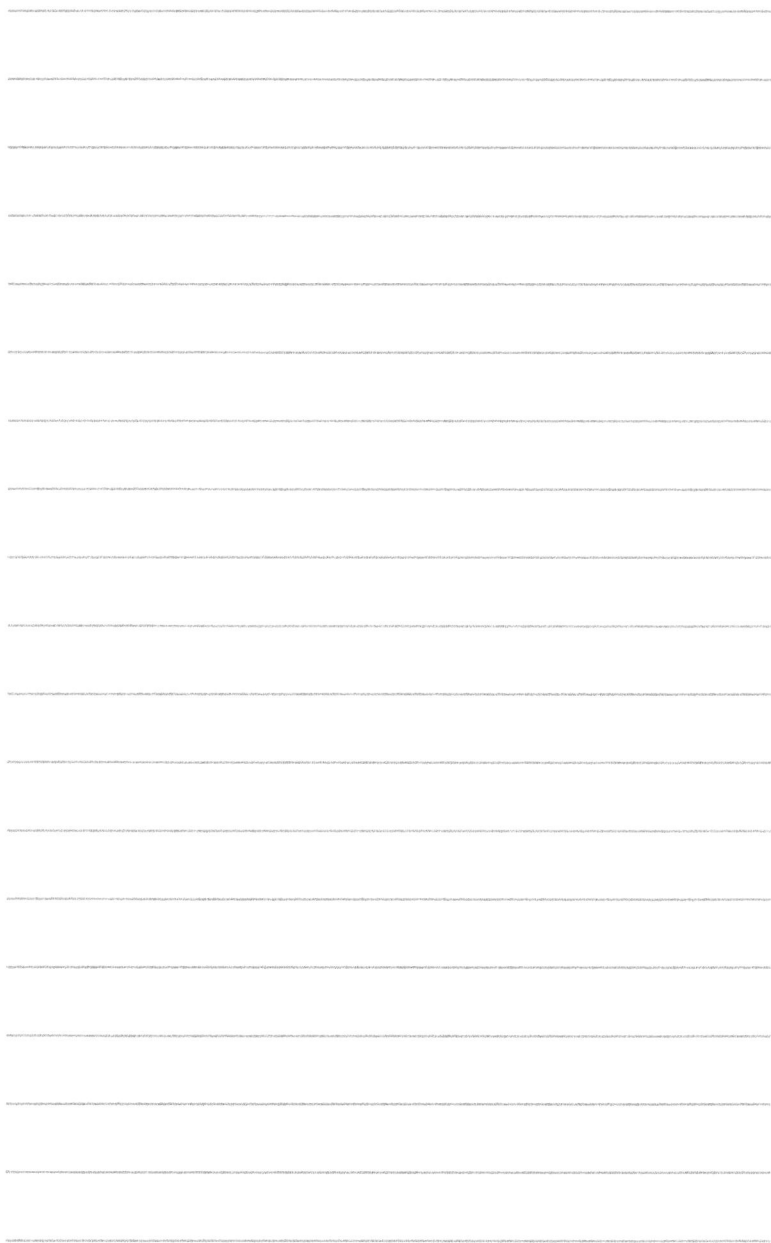

www.ingramcontent.com/pod-product-compliance
Lightning Source LLC
LaVergne TN
LVHW051206080426
835508LV00021B/2843